THE RESEARCH METHOD
IN SOCIAL WORK EDUCATION

# The Research Method
# in Social Work Education

SAMUEL MENCHER, 1918-1967,

## *VOLUME IX*

A Project Report of the Curriculum Study
Werner W. Boehm, Director and Coordinator

COUNCIL ON SOCIAL WORK EDUCATION
345 EAST 46TH STREET, NEW YORK 17, N. Y.

60

Printed in the United States of America
by H. Wolff Book Manufacturing Co., Inc.

## PROJECT DIRECTOR

Samuel Mencher, D.S.W.
*Graduate School of Social Work*
*University of Pittsburgh*
*Pittsburgh, Pennsylvania*

v

## PUBLISHER'S NOTE

### Board Policy

This project report of the Curriculum Study is published in accordance with the policy adopted by the Board of Directors of the Council at its meeting on October 9–11, 1958. The policy adopted provides that:

The content of Curriculum Study reports are the responsibility of the Curriculum Study staff;

These reports will be published by the Council as submitted to it by the Study staff and given the widest possible distribution;

The Council, through all possible channels, shall encourage thorough consideration and discussion of the findings and recommendations and their implications for social work education and practice.

The Board decided further that:

Publication and distribution of the Curriculum Study reports does not imply Council acceptance of the findings or recommendations;

Implementation of any of the recommendations of the Study can come only after the field has had full opportunity to consider the reports, the appropriate bodies of the Council have considered and recommended action which would modify or change existing policies and standards.

The Board sincerely hopes that the many challenging questions which the Study presents will be given the mature, deliberate and objective consideration they merit and which characterize the true profession.

The Board wishes to register on behalf of the Council its sincere appreciation to the Study staff whose dedicated service brought the Curriculum Study to a successful conclusion.

The thirteen volumes of the Curriculum Study have been numbered to facilitate reference and identification. The comprehensive report has been numbered Volume I, the report on undergraduate education because of its comprehensive nature has been numbered Volume II. The other volumes have been numbered in alphabetical order by title as follows:

## Acknowledgments

The Board is pleased to make public acknowledgment of its appreciation to the following foundations and organizations whose grants made possible the financing of this Curriculum Study:

FIELD FOUNDATION

ITTLESON FAMILY FOUNDATION

NATIONAL INSTITUTE OF MENTAL HEALTH, DEPARTMENT OF HEALTH, EDUCATION, AND WELFARE

NATIONAL TUBERCULOSIS ASSOCIATION

NEW YORK FUND FOR CHILDREN

OFFICE OF VOCATIONAL REHABILITATION, DEPARTMENT OF HEALTH, EDUCATION, AND WELFARE

ROCKEFELLER BROTHERS FUND

Although all projects of the Curriculum Study were interdependent and each contributed to the others and to the comprehensive report—and the staff worked as a team under one director—certain grants were more particularly earmarked for designated projects. Accordingly, acknowledgment is made of this circumstance in the appropriate volumes.

In addition to grants from these organizations, the Council on Social Work Education made substantial contributions from its own funds.

—Ernest F. Witte

*New York, New York*  *Executive Director*

*May, 1959*   *Council on Social Work Education*

# Preface

This comprehensive three-year study of curriculum in the education of social workers has been completed under the auspices of the Council on Social Work Education. It has comprised twelve separate projects, one of which is reported in the following pages.

The twelve individual project reports are published separately by the Council to meet the needs of social work educators and practitioners whose interest is especially concentrated in the subject matter of one or more of the projects. No single report, however, can be understood in its proper relation to the whole study without reference to the comprehensive report, *Objectives for the Social Work Curriculum of the Future,* in which the findings and recommendations of the total study are presented. The various project directors worked together as a staff under the over-all guidance of Dr. Werner W. Boehm, Director and Coordinator of the Curriculum Study. Their goal was not only to develop desirable educational objectives for each project's particular area of the curriculum or suggested by particular considerations of practice, but, in addition, to do so in a way that would merge them all into a total educational experience.

Each project was designed to fit into a master plan for the study of the total curriculum. The findings and recommendations of each are relevant to those of the whole Study and have in turn been influenced by all other projects. To be understood, each report must therefore be considered in relation to the comprehensive report, which it supplements by supplying details for the particular area of the social work curriculum.

## WHY THE STUDY WAS UNDERTAKEN

Many issues facing social work education were identified in the Hollis-Taylor Report of 1951.[1] It confirmed that the great preponderance of persons engaged in social work activities were still without professional education. It raised such questions as:

Does social work have a well-defined and identified function?

Does it possess a systematic body of knowledge, skills and attitudes in the various areas of social work practice?

Is the content of social work education sufficiently well developed so that it can be transmitted, and is it of such caliber that it can be included properly as a professional discipline within a university?

Progress toward answering these questions was made by the adoption of the Council's Curriculum Policy Statement in 1952, but further study was indicated. Social work education had also to face other issues:

How could it meet the greatly increased need for social work personnel?

How best could it train for a professional practice still in the process of rapid change and development? Can it be broad enough in scope to enable social workers to function in fields just emerging as well as those already established? Will breadth of education to encompass all fields of professional practice result in dilution of competence for specific fields?

How could it inculcate qualities of leadership and statesmanship while at the same time training for competence in specific practice?

Should undergraduate education serve primarily as a basis for graduate training or also prepare personnel for certain social work positions?

The Study considered that materials from which answers to all these questions might emerge would be obtained by focusing upon

[1] Ernest V. Hollis and Alice L. Taylor, *Social Work Education in the United States* (New York: Columbia University Press, 1951).

fundamental questions of curriculum planning and not by piece-meal consideration of the specific questions posed. In education for social work as for other professions, the fundamental considerations in curriculum planning apply, as presented succinctly by Dr. Ralph W. Tyler.[2] Paraphrased for purposes of this study they are:

What are the desirable educational objectives for professional education?

What learning experiences should be selected and devised and how organized, to realize these objectives?

What are the effective means of evaluating whether the objectives have been attained?

Without a clear formulation of the objectives of social work education, that is, the knowledge, skills and attitudes students are expected to acquire, it becomes impossible to plan the learning experiences needed or to evaluate their success. Consequently, the Curriculum Study singled out as its major task identification of the desirable objectives of social work education.

Also, in accordance with Dr. Tyler's definition, each project framed its educational objectives in terms of both the *content* to be covered and the kind and quality of *behavior* to be expected from the student in relation to the content. For example, "familiarity" with a certain area of content becomes distinguishable from behaviors involving more complex manipulations or deeper "understanding" of content at other levels of student learning.

## HOW THE STUDY WAS CARRIED ON

The individual projects of the study fell into the following major areas:

1. Specific curriculum areas—projects devised to examine the curriculum in the areas identified by the Curriculum Policy Statement of 1952: Human Growth and Behavior, the Social

2 Ralph W. Tyler, *Basic Principles of Curriculum and Instruction* (Chicago: The University of Chicago Press, 1950).

Services, Social Work Methods (casework, group work, community organization, research, administration).

2. Selected fields of practice—projects devised to study elements of practice in rehabilitation, public social services, and corrections.
3. Undergraduate education for social work.
4. Content on social work values and ethics found throughout the curriculum.

Each project was planned to identify educational objectives in existing curricula; to formulate a series of desirable objectives, the desirability of which was determined by judging their importance, consistency and compatibility with a statement of the nature and function of social work; and to review the objectives in the light of educational theory as to the possibility of their being learned in the time and conditions available. Project directors had consultation and assistance from specially selected panels of educators and practitioners in social work and related disciplines.

## WHAT THE STUDY HOPES TO ACCOMPLISH

Responsibility for planning and constructing curriculum belongs basically to the social work schools and departments. As a group they have already come far toward definition of common educational goals for the profession and of content all curricula must have to reach such goals. The Curriculum Study is expected to provide guides for the resolution of the major issues and common questions that it is anticipated will arise in the curriculum planning of all member schools and departments of the Council on Social Work Education.

# Contents

THE RESEARCH METHOD
IN SOCIAL WORK EDUCATION

# CHAPTER I

# Social Work Roles Related to Research

The purpose of the study of the research area of the social work curriculum has been to formulate desirable educational objectives and to suggest related learning experiences for the training of master's students preparing for practice in fields other than social work research. In general, the definition of research curriculum objectives for students preparing to engage in the "service" methods has centered about: (1) the contribution which learning in research can make to the practitioner's skill in his own method; and (2) the contribution which the practitioner can be expected to make to the development of research knowledge. These are not sharply separable goals, since the capacities required for effective performance of one frequently overlap those of the other. Both contributions are, however, difficult to define with precision. In the case of the first, the influence of the research curriculum can be gauged only indirectly as it affects the practice of another method. In the case of the second, the practitioner's role, whether directly or indirectly related to research, varies greatly. On the whole, though, the kinds of behavior toward which the research component has been expected to contribute have been found wanting, both in the practitioner's own method and in his relationship to research.

The initial problem then, in formulating desirable objectives, is the clarification of the contribution which the research area of the curriculum can make to the total professional equipment of students preparing for social work practice in other than research positions. Therefore, the professional tasks of the practitioner have been examined in terms of the attitudes, knowledge and skills for which research teaching may be expected to assume some responsibility.

The plan of this study has been to distinguish roles and sub-roles for whose preparation the research content is significant, and to define the capacities within these roles for which educational objectives may be delineated. Three major roles have been distinguished:

**I. The Practitioner of a Service Method**
**II. The Research Practitioner**
**III. The Research Specialist**

This study will be concerned only with preparation for the former two roles.[1] The roles of practitioner and research-practioner vary *relatively* rather than *absolutely* in their relationship to research. The primary skill of both is a "service" method, and both may participate in research undertakings. However, there appears to be a definite and growing need for the practitioner who renders service as part of a research design, a practitioner who, as Isaac L. Hoffman states, has a "research orientation." [2] This type of worker, because of greater interest in research and with additional knowledge gained from training and experience, may also take leadership in small agency studies or seek advanced preparation for the role of research specialist. It would seem advisable as well as possible that curriculum objectives and learning experiences be arranged to prepare some workers for this role without appreciable changes in the regular curriculum.[3] On the other hand, in view of the already overcrowded master's curriculum, differences in interest among students in research, and the limited opportunities for such activity, it would not seem an objective to be considered for all practitioners.[4] In the analysis of sub-roles, capacities and objectives, those

[1] The exclusion of the research specialist from this study has not been determined by the appropriateness or lack of appropriateness of the master's curriculum for training research specialists, but rather by the limits of the study, *i.e.* curriculum planning for master's students whose primary professional training is in one of the "service" methods.
[2] Unpublished memorandum to members of the Committee on Research Functions and Practice of the Social Work Research Group. This organization will be referred to in this report as SWRG.
[3] B. R. Buckingham suggests a similar goal for primary and secondary school teachers. He uses the term "research teachers," and is of the opinion that "at least for a selected few teachers" this opportunity be provided. See "The Value of Research to Teachers," *The Implications of Research for the Classroom Teacher,* Joint Yearbook American Educational Research Association and the Department of Classroom Teachers (Washington, D.C.: National Education Association of the United States, 1939), 24–37.
[4] This approach differs from much of current curriculum planning in research which either seeks to prepare all practitioners for every possible contingency requiring research knowledge or structures distinct research specializations.

suggested for the practitioner generally will be considered relevant for the research-practitioner as well.

## I. THE ROLE OF PRACTITIONER OF A SERVICE METHOD

The role of practitioner has been divided into four sub-roles for the purpose of delineating specific capacities toward which the research component may be expected to contribute. These have been developed and refined in the light of the following source materials: current curriculum objectives of schools of social work, workshop reports on research and education for research, memoranda of the Social Work Research Section of the National Association of Social Workers, reports on research projects, the general literature of the field, and a survey of a selected sample of research specialists in contact with practitioners in research.

In enumerating the four sub-roles, two mentioned with varying frequency have been omitted: consumer of research and independent researcher. The first has not been included because it is contained within the roles cited and because the term consumer suggests, at least in American society, a passive rather than an active role.

In regard to the role of independent researcher, while only three schools specifically referred to this goal, the curriculum of several other schools made it possible to infer this expectation. The approach of this study has been that the master's curriculum for the practitioner of service methods does not present a realistic opportunity for preparing practitioners to undertake research independently, and that the inclusion of this objective tends to confuse curriculum planning.[5]

[5] This point of view is in agreement with recent workshop reports on research in the master's curriculum and with a report prepared for SWRG by Sophie T. Cambria and Alfred J. Kahn. The authors state, "Teachers of social work research have not labored under the misconception that research at the master's level provides training for competence and skill in the *doing* of research. The preparation of research specialists remains the task of either a specialization at the master's level or post-graduate work in the field of research." (*The Research Component at the Master's Level,* A Report to a Special SWRG Committee, December 1954, unpublished.)

There has, of course, even been question as to the value of specialized master's

The purpose of the approach in this study is neither to discourage nor to deny the possibility of research being undertaken by the master's graduate, but rather to set limits for curriculum planning which will promote most effectively the learning needs of the large body of students within the general master's program. It is the opinion of the author that at least some of the difficulty in curriculum planning has been the result of the conflict, albeit frequently not clearly defined, between preparing practitioners and preparing researchers.

The following roles for practitioners of a service method have been distinguished in relation to the research sequence as focal points for the planning of curriculum objectives:

## I. Practitioner of a Service Method

    A. PRACTITIONER PROVIDING SERVICE THROUGH HIS OWN METHOD
    B. PRACTITIONER PARTICIPATING IN RESEARCH
    C. PRACTITIONER FUNCTIONING AS STAFF MEMBER OF AGENCY
    D. PRACTITIONER ACTING AS MEMBER OF A PROFESSION

Although these roles are not mutually exclusive and do not necessarily require different curriculum objectives, they do provide stable points around which to structure capacities and define objectives. For each of the four roles, capacities relevant to their fulfillment through the research component of the curriculum have been organized. The capacities, like the roles, have been suggested by the sources cited above. The roles themselves have also indicated additional capacities. Preparation for all the capacities is not necessarily either the sole or the major responsibility of the research curriculum, but the capacities are generally those for which the research component has taken some responsibility. After the capacities have been delineated, more specific curriculum objectives will be suggested. This approach, aside from being a means of developing curriculum objectives, also offers the possibility for those planning specific curricula to distinguish the most desirable among the role objectives and to balance or organize their curricula to this end.

---

sequences in research. The 1951 Research Workshop of the American Association of Schools of Social Work, for example, expressed the opinion that "only beginners could be trained at the master's level" in a specialized sequence.

RESEARCH-RELATED CAPACITIES OF THE PRACTITIONER PROVIDING
SERVICE THROUGH HIS OWN METHOD (ROLE I A) [6]

1. Ability to apply logical and orderly thinking to problems presented in own practice.
2. Attitude of scientific inquiry toward own practice.
3. Willingness to question the theory and method upon which own practice is based.
4. Ability to organize and present own practice experience objectively and clearly.[7]
5. Interest in the growing body of knowledge related to own practice.
6. Appreciation of the contribution that research can make to the field of practice.
7. Ability to evaluate critically new contributions to method and theory of practice.
8. Acquaintance with sources of research knowledge about practice.
9. Acquaintance with sources of data related to problems confronted in own practice.
10. Ability to evaluate, analyze and draw conclusions from statistical data.[8]

In Chart I A on page 10, these capacities are summarized. The left-hand column lists briefly four major areas into which the ca-

[6] See Appendix, Table I, for the number of schools emphasizing these capacities in their curricula.

[7] See William E. Gordon, "The Challenge of Research to Today's Medical Social Worker," *Social Work,* I (January, 1956). Gordon discusses the responsibility of the practitioner for awareness of his own practice and its problems and for articulating clearly and systematically about the "knowledge" on which "practice is based."

James B. Conant describes the circular relationship between science and technology during the war as "a continuous chain running from the laboratory to the battlefield." The practitoner being on the "battlefield" of social work must maintain "the reverse flow of information, suggestions, and demands moving smoothly to the development groups and the laboratories." (*Science and Common Sense* [New Haven: Yale University Press, 1951], 305–15.)

[8] See John S. Morgan, "The Research Component in Social Work Education," *Social Work Research,* Subject Area IV Workshop Report, 1954 *Proceedings*—Annual Program Meeting, Council on Social Work Education (New York: CSWE, 1954), 10 ff. In a recent survey of group work graduates, one of the major suggestions for the research and statistics course was training in the use of statistics in daily agency practice, *e.g.,* census material, agency and community surveys. Gladys Ryland, *Employment Responsibilities of Social Group Work Graduates* (New York: CSWE, 1958), 46, 49.

pacities can be grouped as to *content*. The headings across the top represent the major types of *behavior* to be expected from the student with respect to each content area. This breakdown of the capacities required for each role follows the Tyler framework of the whole Curriculum Study. It enables this project to derive from the roles and their related capacities the specific educational objectives recommended for the research area of the curriculum. Charts I B, I C, and I D similarly summarize the content and behaviors of capacities required for those sub-roles, and Chart II performs the same function for the role of research-practitioner. Chart III puts all these summaries of role capacities into tabulated form and serves as a basis for derivation of more specific educational objectives in Chapter II.

For the purpose of standardizing the behavioral aspects of the curriculum objectives, the following terms will be used:

*Critical thinking* is a combination of attitudes toward scientific inquiry and abilities in systematic problem-solving. Such attitudes as disciplined curiosity, appreciation of the tentativeness of knowledge, willingness to re-examine currently accepted methods and theories and to accept change on the basis of evidence, and appreciation of objective findings as fundamental to problem-solving, are at the core of critical thinking.[9]

Critical thinking abilities are a combination of inductive, deductive and logical thinking. In problem-solving critical thinking involves: "identifying basic assumptions, thinking in an orderly manner (progressing from one conclusion to another in meaningful sequence, and arranging premises, assumptions and conclusions to develop a rational argument); distinguishing between relevant and irrelevant ideas, distinguishing between conclusions which follow and those which do not follow from a given set of assumptions, and formulating thoughtful pertinent questions that can be answered." [10]

[9] K. R. Popper uses the apt phrase "horizon of expectations" to describe the way the scientist constantly brings to bear attitudes or expectations on the situation. Progress in problem-solving occurs when some fact "makes a hole" in these expectations and necessitates "the formation of a new horizon." John Oulton Wisdom, *Foundations of Inference in Natural Science* (London: Methuen and Co., 1952), 7–8.
[10] Ole Sande, *Curriculum Study in Basic Nursing Education* (New York: G. P. Putnam's Sons, 1955), 33.

The following elements are generally identified with critical thinking skills in problem-solving: (1) the ability to define a problem; (2) the ability to select pertinent information for the solution of a problem; (3) the ability to recognize stated and unstated assumptions; (4) the ability to formulate and select relevant and promising hypotheses; and (5) the ability to draw conclusions validly and to judge the validity of inferences.[11]

The ability to apply conclusions, to evaluate conclusions in terms of their application and to take action after critical consideration, is also frequently included as an element of critical thinking. However, in this report it has been treated as a separate ability.

*Acquaintance* means an idea of the major considerations involved in the subject area but not in great detail.

*Appreciation* means sufficient information in the subject area to be able to isolate the importance of the subject and the major problems in the area.

*Knowledge* means sufficient information of the subject area to recognize the doctrine, principles, procedures, and so on, and to deal in matters which are effected by the subject. Not detailed enough to allow competency without further study or research in the subject area.

*Understanding* means sufficient knowledge of a subject area to be able to use the knowledge as a basis for further study or application either at the school or later. Sufficient knowledge to be able to recognize the interrelationship of forces acting within, or on, the subject area.

*Ability to apply* means an understanding, knowledge or skill sufficient to assure an effective performance or a satisfactory conclusion.[12]

11 Paul L. Dressel and Lewis B. Mayhew, *General Education, Explorations in Evaluation* (Washington, D.C.: American Council on Education, 1954), 179–180. This entire volume is a study of education for critical thinking. Other sources on critical thinking: Ralph W. Tyler, *Basic Principles of Curriculum and Instruction* (Chicago: University of Chicago Press, 1950), 38. Samuel Finestone, "The Scientific Component in the Casework Field Curriculum," *Social Casework*, XXXVI, 5 (May, 1955), 195–202.
12 The terms and their definitions from "acquaintance" through "ability to apply" are those used by Ralph W. Tyler in *Analysis of the Purpose, Pattern, Scope and Structure of the Officer Education Program of Air University,* Technical Memorandum OERL–TM–55–6, Officer Education Research Laboratory. (Mimeo) footnote to page 94.

CHART I A

## Content and Behaviors in Capacities Required for Practitioner in Own Method

| | Behaviors | | | |
| Content | Critical Thinking | Acquaintance with Sources | Appreciation of Function | Ability to Apply to Practice |
|---|---|---|---|---|
| Own Practice * | x | | | |
| Theory and Method of Practice † | x | | | |
| Research in Social Work | x | x | x | x |
| Statistical Data | x | x | | x |

NOTE: Behaviors in Capacities 1, 2, 3, 4, 5, 7, and 10, listed on pages 5 and 6 (of ms.), have been subsumed under the behavior "critical thinking." The Intercollege Committee on Communications Objectives of the Cooperative Study of Evaluation in General Education of the American Council on Education concluded that the "basic element" of communication was the ability to think critically. Dressel and Mayhew, *op. cit.*, 101.

* "Own Practice" refers to the actual, specific performance of the individual practitioner on the job.

† "Theory and Method of Practice" refers to the knowledge, techniques and values which provide the professional base for the practitioner's approach to his "own practice."

RESEARCH RELATED CAPACITIES OF THE
PRACTITIONER PARTICIPATING IN RESEARCH (ROLE I B) [13]

1. Ability to recognize the existence of problems in practice.
2. Ability to define problems of practice.
3. Willingness to question theory and method of practice.
4. Knowledge of the contribution of research to practice.
5. Knowledge of the research approach to problem-solving.
6. Ability to communicate with research specialist.
7. Ability to adapt service skills to the needs of research.
8. Ability to evaluate reliability and validity of own data, or data collected for research personnel.

[13] See Table I for the number of schools emphasizing these capacities in their curricula.

9. Ability to make judgments on data on the basis of own professional knowledge.
10. Ability to evaluate the results of research.
11. Ability to apply research findings in practice.
12. Appreciation of the organization and administration of research in a social agency.[14]

The survey of a selected sample of members of the Social Work Research Section, NASW, indicated that social work practitioners participating in research either function or are expected to function in almost all aspects of research. However, the tasks most frequently performed by, or expected of, practitioners are those most clearly related to the practitioner's knowledge and skill in his own method. (See Appendix, Table II.) Of these, the one performed by far the least adequately has been the defining of problems of practice for research. Although practitioners were less frequently called upon to perform more technical research operations, they showed several marked lacks in these functions. However, the extent to which the practitioner may be prepared within the master's curriculum to perform these tasks adequately is questionable. This point of view seems reflected in the responses of the research specialists to the type of content to be included in the research curriculum for the preparation of practitioners to function in relation to research activities. Here, aside from formulation of research problems and conclusion drawing (essentially critical thinking capacities), training in research methods received less emphasis than other aspects of research content. (See Appendix, Table III.) Thus *Knowledge* of research methods is suggested in Chart I B. This competence may, of course, be supported by other capacities required of the practitioner in respect to his own method, such as critical thinking and the ability to analyze social statistics.

---

[14] This content was rated low for both participants in research and practitioners generally in the survey of research specialists. However, reports of research studies frequently mention the problems of conducting research within social agencies. See particularly, J. Mc V. Hunt, "A Social Agency as a Setting for Research—The Institute of Welfare Research," *Journal of Consulting Psychology*, XIII (April 1949); John Frings, "Research and the Service Agency," Parts I and II, *Social Casework*, XXXI (February and March, 1950).

CHART I B

**Content and Behaviors in Capacities Required for Practitioner Participating in Research**

| Content | | Behaviors | | | | |
|---|---|---|---|---|---|---|
| | *Critical Thinking* | *Knowledge of Purpose and Contribution* | *Knowledge of Method* | *Ability to Apply Practice* | *Ability to Apply to Practice* | *Appreciation of Organization and Administration* |
| Own Practice | x | | | | | |
| Theory and Method of Practice | x | | | | | |
| Research in Social Work | x | x | x | x | x | x |

NOTE: Capacities 1, 2, 3, 8, 9, 10, listed on page 9 (in ms.), have been included under critical thinking, Capacity 6 under critical thinking and knowledge of research method.

RESEARCH-RELATED CAPACITIES OF PRACTITIONER
FUNCTIONING AS STAFF MEMBER OF AGENCY (ROLE I C)

1. Understanding the purpose of agency fact-finding studies.
2. Knowledge of the method of data collection in social agencies for fact-finding purposes.
3. Ability to formulate questions pertinent to own practice and agency policy.
4. Ability to critically evaluate data resulting from agency studies and to draw conclusions pertinent to agency practice and policy.
5. Ability to interpret or communicate data from agency studies to those interested in agency operations.

CHART I C

**Content and Behaviors in Capacities Required for Practitioner Functioning As Staff Member of Agency**

| | Behaviors | | |
| --- | --- | --- | --- |
| *Content* | *Critical Thinking* | *Understanding Function* | *Knowledge of Method* |
| Agency Fact-finding Studies | x | x | x |
| Own Practice | x | | |
| Policy-making | x | | |

RESEARCH-RELATED CAPACITIES OF PRACTITIONER
AS MEMBER OF PROFESSION (ROLE I-D)

1. Appreciation of the function of research.
2. Ability to evaluate critically contributions to knowledge in own field.
3. Acquaintance with the organization and administration of research in the profession generally.
4. Critical thinking in regard to problems of professional policy.
5. Ability to communicate own practice experience.

CHART I D

**Content and Behaviors in Capacities Required for Practitioner as Member of Profession**

|  | Behaviors | | |
|---|---|---|---|
| Content | Critical Thinking | Appreciation of Function | Acquaintance with Organization and Administration |
| Own Practice | x | | |
| Research in Social Work | x | x | x |
| Policy-making | x | | |

## II. THE ROLE OF RESEARCH PRACTITIONER

The attitudes, knowledge and skills of the research practitioner include those already delineated in the roles for the practitioner of a service method. However, greater knowledge and skill are suggested in specific aspects of research content.

1. Understanding of the function of research in social work.
2. Understanding of the research method of problem-solving.
3. Knowledge of organization and administration of research in social work.

CHART II

**Content and Behaviors in Capacities Required for Research Practitioner**

|  | Behaviors | | |
|---|---|---|---|
| Content | Understanding of Function | Understanding of Method | Knowledge of Organization and Administration |
| Research in Social Work | x | x | x |

## SUMMARY OF CONTENT AND BEHAVIORS IN CAPACITIES REQUIRED FOR ROLES

The capacities suggested by the roles of practitioner and research practitioner are summarized in Chart III. The clustering of roles around specific content and types of behavior indicates the most salient points for curriculum planning. The next steps in planning are the translation of these general capacities into definite curriculum objectives and consideration of the learning experiences most fruitful for their achievement. However, Chart III reveals several factors which should be examined before constructing specific educational objectives for the research component.

1. *The distribution of objectives between the research sequence and other elements of the curriculum.* It is apparent from Chart III that many of the capacities related to the research component and necessary for the effective performance of its objectives are objectives for other parts of the curriculum. Critical thinking about the social worker's own practice, the theory and method of practice, and policy-making are objectives of the components of the curriculum where this content is learned. Agency fact-finding studies have implications for both research and administration. From the point of view of research, they may be included as one of the types of studies conducted within the field of social work and their methodology analyzed. However, their significance as a tool for effective administration makes them an important element of the content of administration courses.

   A great deal of other content, too, falls between the research component and other areas of the curriculum. Sources of research knowledge, the function of research and its application to practice are fundamental to the specific fields to which research contributes. This is true as well for statistical data. As Helen Witmer has pointed out, one of the major factors impeding the student's interest in research had been the fact that neither teaching nor practice is "research-based." "That being the situation, it seems only natural that . . . students regard research as a kind of extracurricular activity, one that does not have a really vital connection with their education for professional work." [15] Principles of learning indicate, too, that the most successful learning experiences will be found within the components of the curriculum most closely identified with the student's practice and with the kinds of behavior expected of him in practice.[16]

2. *The distinction between research methods and critical thinking.* A distinction is made between critical thinking attitudes and abilities and knowledge or understanding of the research method. The separation of these objectives emphasizes that critical thinking is a behavior which must be related to specific content, including research, rather than a behavior synonymous with the content of the research method. There has been some tendency in curriculum planning to assume that critical thinking is included within or derives from research-mindedness. Aside from the limitations of this approach for student learning, this assumption itself is most questionable. The research method is not categorically identified with critical thinking or even more explicitly, with the so-called "scientific method." [17] As Conant and others have remarked, the latter resembles more an artful manipulation or "tactics and strategy" rather than a rigidly defined system of problem-solving.

3. *Levels of behavioral aspects.* Finally the plan outlined in Chart III indicates different levels of behavioral goals relative to the roles previously analyzed. As noted above, this permits differences in emphasis in accordance with the specific objectives of those doing curriculum planning. In this report

[15] Witmer refers to casework only, but her comment may validly be broadened to include the whole of social work teaching and practice. "Teaching Research Method to Students of Social Casework," (unpublished paper, AASSW, January 1948), 2.

[16] See section on learning experiences below.

[17] Remarking on the difficulty of providing problem-solving experiences in science education for prospective scientists, Sidney J. French states, ". . . we have an already existing order of dogma and ritual together with a strongly entrenched hierarchy. . . . Nevertheless, [there is] the need for radical departure from methods and content that have prevailed for half a century, and that have become so stereotyped as to have lost their spontaneity. . . ." Sidney J. French, "General Education and Special Education in the Sciences," *General Education in Science,* ed. by I. Bernard Cohen and Fletcher G. Watson (Cambridge: Harvard University Press, 1952), 32–3.

CHART III

## Summary of Research-Related Capacities for Roles of Practitioner and Research Practitioner

| Content | Critical Thinking | Acquaintance with Sources of Information | Appreciation (of Function) | Knowledge (of Function) | Understanding (of Function) | Ability to Apply in Practice (of Method) | Knowledge (of Method) | Understanding (of Method) | Ability to Adapt Practice (of Organization and Administration) | Acquaintance (of Organization and Administration) | Appreciation (of Organization and Administration) | Knowledge (of Organization and Administration) |
|---|---|---|---|---|---|---|---|---|---|---|---|---|
| Own Practice | IA, IB, IC, ID | | | | | | | | | | | |
| Theory and Method of Practice | IA, IB | | | | | | | | | | | |
| Research in Social Work | IA, IB, ID | IA | IA, ID | IB | II | IA, IB | IB | II | IB | ID | IB | II |
| Agency Fact-finding | IC | | IC | IC | | | IC | | | | | |
| Policy-making | IC, ID | | | | | | | | | | | |
| Statistical Data | IA | IA | | | | IA | | | | | | |

Key: IA Practioner in his own method
IB Practioner participating in research
IC Practioner functioning as staff member of agency
ID Practioner as member of profession
II Research Practitioner

only two levels of objectives will be structured: (1) objectives fulfilling the needs of all practitioners under "I," and (2) additional objectives for the research practitioner under "II." As indicated in Chart III, the behavioral aspects of the objectives for the research practitioner require a higher level of capacity in research content. The assumption here is that the general master's curriculum can provide a somewhat more intensive learning experience for some students, if the objectives for the whole are realistically set and appropriately distributed throughout the curriculum, without detracting from the professional training in basic service methods. This approach has the advantage of satisfying the interests and needs of the few without requiring that all satisfy similar expectations. It may provide a core of practitioners desirous of working in research settings and possibly of increasing their competence in re-research through experience and further training. However, the objective is not the preparation of any level of research specialist.

# CHAPTER II

# Desirable Educational Objectives for Research Courses

If the content of the capacities summarized in Chart III are examined as to their relevance to the research sequence, three elements fall clearly within the responsibility of the research curriculum: research in social work, agency fact-finding, and statistical data. Since agency fact-finding is fundamentally a category of research employing statistical techniques, this content may be logically included within the content of research and statistics. For purposes of clarification, the content area, research in social work, may be divided between: (1) research as a field of practice about which the practitioner should have some level of knowledge (comparable in some ways to his knowledge of other related specializations); and (2) research as a method requiring attitudes, knowledge and skill related both to the extent of the practitioner's participation in research and to the significance to him as a practitioner of the kinds of knowledge and skill acquired through the research method.

The three areas of content thus delineated—research in social work, research methods, and statistics—conform to three of the four basic elements of content currently emphasized in the research curricula of schools of social work.[1] The fourth area presently included in curricula, the general nature of science and the scientist's approach to problem-solving, would not normally appear to be the concern of a graduate curriculum.[2] However, its essentiality to

[1] See Appendix, Table IV.

[2] American Association of Schools of Social Work, *Research in Social Work*, Workshop Report, Annual Program Meeting, 1950 (New York: CSWE, mimeo #2051), 5. The assumption in this study is that undergraduate training takes responsibility for a systematic, integrated and well-rounded general education. Preparation in logical thinking, principles of the scientific approach, and statistical reasoning are fundamental to the goals of general education, no matter what the specific interest of the student or the content emphasized. Failure to develop and to apply these abilities at

understanding the nature and function of research, the relationship of practice to research, the significance of critical thinking generally, as well as the place of the social work profession in "an increasingly science-oriented culture," [3] makes it necessary for this background to be provided for those currently entering schools of social work who are inadequately prepared. The emphasis placed on this content, both for participants in research and practitioners generally, by the research specialists surveyed (see Appendix, Table III) supports the continuance of this content in current curriculum planning.

Major problems, however, center about the factors to be included under the four areas of content and the weight to be given each of the areas in the total sequence. In view of the concentration of roles (Chart III) on the objectives of critical thinking and the nature of research in social work rather than on methods and statistics, more weight has been given the former in the present study. This approach is in general agreement with the relatively greater stress placed on these aspects of the research curriculum by the sample of research specialists. One of the fundamental questions for the research component is the degree of responsibility to be taken for the common goal of critical thinking. Although critical thinking has been approached as a common behavioral objective for all sequences, the great need of practitioners for this capacity and the present limitations of other components of the curriculum with respect to it probably give the research sequence a greater responsibility for critical thinking than it might otherwise have, or can fulfill successfully.

Thus the research sequence has a dual objective toward critical thinking: (1) laying the foundation for critical thinking by including the principles and elements which underlie problem-solving generally in a "science-oriented culture;" and (2) applying critical

---

the undergraduate level will have the effect of negating much of the value of the undergraduate curriculum and consequently of providing the professional school with a candidate poorly equipped to deal with professional content. In addition, there is strong likelihood that the student who has not developed capacities generally associated with critical thinking by the completion of his undergraduate training, will have acquired patterns of problem-solving which will be extremely difficult to correct.

[3] William E. Gordon, *Toward Basic Research in Social Work* (St. Louis: Washington University, 1951), 17.

thinking attitudes and abilities to the content of social work research. The research sequence provides the basic elements common
to all scientifically oriented problem-solving. This, however, does
not relieve the other sequences of relating and organizing these
elements with reference to their own content. The difference of
approach of the research component may be more clearly viewed
if the elements of critical thinking are delineated in the content of
the objectives of the research sequence whereas they are essentially
behavioral aspects of the other sequences.

It is for this reason that critical thinking is not included in the
behavioral aspects of the objectives suggested for the research curriculum, and the essential factors necessary for critical thinking are
delineated in the content areas, scientific method and problem-
solving through the research method. This approach also supports
a clearer determination of what is actually involved in so complex
(and frequently so vaguely defined) a behavior as critical thinking.
It should be noted, however, that the attitudes identified with
critical thinking are a necessary adjunct of the levels of knowledge
and skill suggested in the objectives.

When critical thinking is applied to research content, the research curriculum, like other sequences, must orient the student to
its own assumptions and strategy and develop criteria applicable
to research undertakings.[4]

The curriculum objectives suggested as desirable for the research sequence are focused around four major content areas:

A. Scientific Method
B. Problem-solving through the Research Method
C. Research in Social Work
D. Statistics

These content areas are defined and related to appropriate behavioral expectations. The behavioral aspects of the objectives are
those used in the analysis of roles above. They provide a rough
scale of capacities and are supplemented by the extensity of content
which indicates the relative weight given the elements of the re-

[4] Council on Social Work Education, "Research in Social Agencies—Implications for
the Teaching of Social Work Students," in *Social Work Research, op. cit.,* 3.

search sequence. Thus, in comparing the four areas above, research in social work and problem-solving through the research method have received greatest emphasis, as may be noted from examination of both the extensity of content and levels of behavioral aspects of the objectives.

| Content | Behavior |
| --- | --- |
| A.  Scientific Method | |
|    1. The Purpose of Scientific Inquiry . . . . . . . . . . . | Appreciation |
|    2. Relationship of Science and Technology . . . . . | Appreciation |
|    3. Characteristics of Scientific Approach | |
|      a. Principles or Assumptions of Scientist [5] . . . . | Understanding |
|        Causality . . . . . . . . . . . . . . . . . . . . . . . . . . . . . . . | " |
|        Consistency . . . . . . . . . . . . . . . . . . . . . . . . . | " |
|        Uniformity . . . . . . . . . . . . . . . . . . . . . . . . . | " |
|        Simplicity . . . . . . . . . . . . . . . . . . . . . . . . . | " |
|        Tentativeness . . . . . . . . . . . . . . . . . . . . . . . | " |
|        Continuous discovery . . . . . . . . . . . . . . . . . . | " |
|        Social limitation . . . . . . . . . . . . . . . . . . . . . . . | " |
|        Objectivity . . . . . . . . . . . . . . . . . . . . . . . . . | " |
|        Relativeness . . . . . . . . . . . . . . . . . . . . . . . | " |
|        Practicality . . . . . . . . . . . . . . . . . . . . . . . | " |
|        Complimentarity . . . . . . . . . . . . . . . . . . . . | " |
|        Dynamism . . . . . . . . . . . . . . . . . . . . . . . . . | " |
|        Continuity . . . . . . . . . . . . . . . . . . . . . . . . . . . | " |
| | |
|      b. Methods of Scientist [5] . . . . . . . . . . . . . . . . . | Understanding |
|        Theory-building . . . . . . . . . . . . . . . . . . . . . . . | " |
|        Hypothesis testing . . . . . . . . . . . . . . . . . . . . | " |
|        Logical reasoning . . . . . . . . . . . . . . . . . . . . | " |
|        Empirical design . . . . . . . . . . . . . . . . . . . . | " |
|        Abstraction . . . . . . . . . . . . . . . . . . . . . . . | " |
|        Generalization . . . . . . . . . . . . . . . . . . . . . | " |
|        Quantification . . . . . . . . . . . . . . . . . . . . . . | " |

[5] The illustrations given are not meant to exhaust the subject matter under these categories, but merely to denote the types of content to be included. They do, on the whole, represent those most frequently suggested in research courses of the schools of social work as well as the literature on scientific method. It would be desirable to delineate those principles and methods most deserving of greater emphasis within the social work research sequence.

| Content | Behavior | |
| --- | --- | --- |
| | *For Practitioner* | *For Research Practitioner* |
| B. Problem-solving through the Research Method | (Role I) | (Role II) |
| 1. Problem Definition | Ability | Ability |
| Problem Recognition ......... | " | " |
| Problem Identification ........ | " | " |
| 2. Solution Formulation | Ability | Ability |
| Location of sources of information ..................... | " | " |
| Evaluation of information ..... | " | " |
| Systematization of information . | " | " |
| Development of promising solutions ................. | " | " |
| 3. Solution Exploration or Testing | | |
| Research Design ............. | Appreciation | Knowledge |
| Data Collection | | |
| General methods .......... | Appreciation | Knowledge |
| Methods involving social work skills [6] ................. | Ability | Ability |
| Organization, classification, analysis ................ | Knowledge | Knowledge |
| 4. Conclusion Drawing ........... | Ability | Ability |
| Validity .................... | " | " |
| Applicability .............. | " | " |
| 5. Reporting .................... | Ability | Ability |

---

[6] In regard to the relationship between data collection and practice, see Edna Levy Wasser, "The Caseworker as Research Interviewer in Follow-up Studies," *Social Casework*, XXXVIII (October 1957). Also, Gertrude Wilson, *Membership Intake for What*, A Report of Four Studies Which Grow Out of the Analysis of the Content and Process of Membership Registration Interviews at the Educational Alliance, 1950–51 (duplicated and available from the Educational Alliance, New York). Both these reports delineate the role of the practitioner in collecting data. The latter presents the difficulties of practitioners in focusing interviews for specific information and in recording "definite facts and judgments without the protection of descriptive verbiage." Experience in this type of data collection offers opportunities for sharpening observation and recording in the practitioner's own method as well.

The approach in Content Areas A and B suggests concentration on the general problem-solving or the methodological rather than the technical aspects of research. The "techniques" or "specific procedures" by which the researcher "gathers and orders his data prior to their logical and statistical manipulation" are given relatively less emphasis in the behavioral aspects of the chart.[7] In data analysis, the emphasis is on logical rather than statistical manipulation. The level of statistical knowledge expected is of the kind needed to analyze statistical data in relation to the practitioner's normal professional responsibilities.

The prominence given the general rather than technical aspects of problem-solving is largely in keeping with the responses of the research specialists (see Appendix, Table III). Formulation of research problems and conclusion drawing were considered to be particularly essential aspects of content for the practitioner participating in research. The abilities stressed in relation to the total content above are those broadly required in critical thinking by the practitioner on his own job and as a consumer of data, literature and research findings in the professional field.

| Content | Behavior | |
| --- | --- | --- |
| | *For Practitioner* | *For Research Practitioner* |
| C. Research in Social Work | (Role I) | (Role II) |
| 1. Function and objectives ...... | Knowledge | Understanding |
| 2. Relationship of research in social work to practice ........... | Knowledge | Understanding |
| 3. Relationship of social work practice to other sources of research knowledge ............... | Acquaintance | Acquaintance |
| 4. Sources of research knowledge ... | Acquaintance | Acquaintance |
| 5. Organization and administration | Appreciation | Knowledge |
| 6. Problems and limitations of research in social work ........ | Appreciation | Knowledge |
| 7. Types of studies undertaken .... | Knowledge | Knowledge |
| 8. Current status and trends ...... | Knowledge | Knowledge |

[7] The distinction between "method" and "technique" is suggested by William J. Goode and Paul K. Hatt, *Methods in Social Research* (New York: McGraw-Hill, 1952), 5–6.

Much of the content in this Area C is indicated by the capacities in Chart III. Such content as the relationship of research in social work and related fields of practice and the sources of research knowledge, may be the primary responsibility of courses identified with specific areas of social work and social science knowledge. However, since general curriculum objectives stress recognition of the place of research in social work and critical consumption of research on the part of the practitioner, a sound general introduction to, or review of, research in social work is appropriate. The practitioner should be aware of the problems and limitations of research and its status and trends. He must have sufficient knowledge of the kinds of problems research is seeking to answer and the direction in which it is heading, if he is to be a sympathetic supporter and constructive critic.[8] He gains professional security from seeing the gains, albeit tentative, from increasing research knowledge. Since one of the problems of practitioners noted by researchers has been expectations of research which research is not ready to fulfill, the practitioner should obtain a realistic view of the status of research.[9]

Through contact with an orderly process of problem-solving, the goals of scientific knowledge, the principles and methods of its development, as well as the immediate issues and problems in social work research, the practitioner is better prepared to participate in research, to recognize its difficulties, understand its values, and critically consider its contribution. Research becomes another method, rather than a complex of intricate and mystifying techniques in which the practitioner has little interest and less capacity.[10]

[8] Charlotte Towle discusses the importance of the student's gaining a sense of continuity of the profession's wisdom in *The Learner in Education for the Professions* (Chicago: The University of Chicago Press, 1954), 278.

[9] Isaac L. Hoffman remarks, "The practitioners expect a far too conclusive result from the simple application of an undeveloped and primitive research process. The end result is that when what passes for research fails to give results of a high order, the practitioner is likely to react negatively to the entire idea of research and scholarship." ("Research, Social Work, and Scholarship," *Social Service Review*, XXX [March, 1956], 23).

[10] It is interesting to note that despite some thirty years of emphasis on research in the social work curriculum attitudes of students have remained very similar to what they were in 1928. See Mildred D. Mudgett, "Research as a Method of Training for Social Work," *Proceedings of the National Conference of Social Work, 1928* (Chicago: The University of Chicago Press, 1928), 554.

| Content | Behavior |
|---|---|
| D. Statistics | |
| 1. Sources of statistical data . . . . . . . . . . . . . . . . . | Acquaintance |
| 2. Statistical measures . . . . . . . . . . . . . . . . . . . . . . | Knowledge |
| Averages . . . . . . . . . . . . . . . . . . . . . . . . . . . . | " |
| Variability . . . . . . . . . . . . . . . . . . . . . . . . . . | " |
| Association . . . . . . . . . . . . . . . . . . . . . . . . . . | " |
| Significance . . . . . . . . . . . . . . . . . . . . . . . . . | " |
| 3. Statistical data organized in tables, charts, graphs . . . . . . . . . . . . . . . . . . . . . . . . | Understanding |
| 4. Statistical concepts . . . . . . . . . . . . . . . . . . . . . | Knowledge |
| Reliability . . . . . . . . . . . . . . . . . . . . . . . . . . | " |
| Validity . . . . . . . . . . . . . . . . . . . . . . . . . . . . | " |
| Randomness . . . . . . . . . . . . . . . . . . . . . . . . . | " |
| Probability . . . . . . . . . . . . . . . . . . . . . . . . . . | " |

It is generally accepted in social work education that basic statistical training is the responsibility of undergraduate preparation. If this were the case, the limited objectives presented above would normally be achieved prior to the student's entering professional training. At present most schools include some statistical content in their research sequence.[11] In some instances courses in statistics receive no credit or are waived when the student has had satisfactory prior training. Recently there has been a growing impression that research courses have "overstressed" the details of statistical methodology and that their content should be geared to the basic theory and logic of statistics and the meaning of measures and concepts rather than a mastery of their application.[12] On the whole, the research specialists in the survey considered statistics the least important content of the research sequence.

[11] Statistical teaching in research courses has varied from "instruction in methods of tabulation, graphic presentation, computation of ratios, rates and percentages, computation of averages and review of sources of social work statistical data to such topics as measures of deviation, time series analysis, index number construction, simple correlation, multiple correlation, chi square and coefficient of contingency, sampling techniques and error." American Association of Schools of Social Work, *Research*, Workshop Report, Annual Program Meeting, 1951 (New York: CSWE, mimeo #2137), 3.
[12] CSWE, "New Developments in Teaching Research in Social Work," in *Social Work Research, op. cit.*, 2.

# CHAPTER III

# Learning Experiences for Research Objectives

Schools of social work generally include in their master's curriculum for all students, regardless of specialization, some sizable requirement in research training. While it is difficult to compare schools because of many variables involved, it has been estimated that master's students spend from 8 or 9 percent to 25 percent of their classroom work in research activity, depending on the school attended.[1] On the whole, this is probably the largest amount of time spent by students in any field other than in courses related to their immediate professional goals.

## ORGANIZATION OF RESEARCH COURSES

Although there is no standard pattern of research training for the master's student not specializing in research, there are approaches common to most schools. Nearly all schools have a one semester general course in research methods during the first year. A large majority arrange this course during the latter part of the first year. A few schools have a full first year introductory course. Several give the introductory course in research methods at the beginning of the second year and combine it with commencement of work on the project. A number of schools whose formal introductory methods course is completed in the first year continue a research sequence with seminar meetings held either throughout the second year project period or during portions of this period. In group or class projects under the guidance of a faculty member, there also tends to be a scheduled series of meetings for instruction, advisement, and coordination.

1 John S. Morgan, "The Research Component in Social Work Education," *Social Work Research*, Subject Area Workshop Report, 1954, Council on Social Work Education, 6.

Some schools give separate courses in statistics as part of the formal research program for all students. In others, statistical content is combined with other research methods in the one- or two-course program. Several schools requiring a course in statistics waive this upon successful completion of an examination or where the student has had sufficient undergraduate training.

## SUMMARY OF EXISTING LEARNING EXPERIENCES

The learning experiences provided students in research will be described first in relation to the formal courses and then in relation to the project. This distinction is for purposes of analysis and does not reflect the frequent practice of planning the two types of learning situations as a unit.

### RESEARCH METHODS COURSES

The breadth of content covered in most research courses does not permit a great variety of learning experiences for the student. The most common teaching techniques are lecture and class discussion supplemented by bibliographic references to the content being considered. In some schools the course outline is in great detail, and issues are sufficiently delineated to stimulate thinking and discussion.

However, a number of other learning situations for active student participation are provided in various schools. The most usual is the *development of an outline or design for a research project* by the student. In most instances, this is done in relation to a problem selected by the student; in a few cases, however, the class as a group constructs a research design and may undertake to complete a small practice research project. While the problems suggested and the designs outlined are not directly related to the student's master's project in many courses, they may form the basis for the student's later research. This latter relationship is found more specifically when the research course is concurrent with the start of the project. Whereas in the first year research methods course, the construction of a research design occurs generally toward the end of the course after the student has had some orientation to research, in the second year course, if the student is to have the whole academic year for project work, the design must come early in the year. This has the advantage of coming when the student is more motivated toward research content.

Some attempts have been made to integrate this experience in research design with other aspects of the student's learning. For example, in one school the class research design is for a project outside the field of social work so that the student may develop a sense of relationship to other disciplines. Another approach has been to have the students follow the research approach in preparing a paper for some other course in the curriculum.

A second type of learning experience participated in by most students in research methods courses is the *analysis of some completed piece or pieces of research*. Specific studies may be analyzed by the group in class, or the students may make individual oral or written reports on selected studies. Selection of studies is based on a number of factors: methodology, subject matter, purpose, administration, or setting of the study. Where several studies are used, they may be arranged to broaden the students' contact with a variety of types of studies; they may emphasize historical perspective by introducing studies from different periods in the development of social work; or they may be organized to meet some criteria related to the general learning needs of the student.[2]

Theses previously completed in the school are used for critical analysis in a few courses. Such studies may have the advantage of not overwhelming the student with highly technical research, and they frequently give greater attention to details of method than is usually the case in published studies. In addition to critical analysis students may prepare abstracts of completed theses or published studies.

Statistical data are also presented for review. Statistical reports of social agencies, national and local, public and private, are ex-

2 For example, one approach is to introduce studies in a logical order—studies of need, studies of meeting need, studies of social workers and their methods, techniques and practices. Richard M. Seaman, "The Case Method in the Teaching and Learning of Social Work Research," *Social Work Journal*, XXXV, 3 (July, 1954), 119–20, 130.

amined. Raw data may also be given the students for organization and interpretation.

The learning experience in some courses is concentrated upon *specific elements of research method*. For example, questions may be posed for which the student must consider the information needed, find the sources, and extract the necessary information. Or the student may be required to develop data collecting instruments, undertake interviews for research purposes, or arrange systems for the classification of data. Each of these elements is usually approached as a discrete learning experience for the purpose of developing specific skills or applying definite principles of the research method of problem-solving. One school with a full year's introductory course has concentrated almost wholly on this approach. However, most research methods courses are too broad in scope and limited in time to employ this method except to a small extent. In general, students in research methods courses have some or a combination of all the learning experiences described above. Where learning of statistics is one of the objectives of the research sequence, the learning situation varies from lecture and discussion to laboratory exercises in statistical techniques. A few schools located near well organized research centers have at times arranged for their students to observe the activities involved in a large scale research undertaking.

THE PROJECT SEMINAR

As already noted, the project seminar (or similar class or group structure) for initiating and, in some schools, following through to completion of the project, has become a widespread practice. Where group projects have already been formulated by the faculty, the meetings of the project group generally replace the seminar. However, when students are selecting their own individual or group projects, the project seminar assists in the selection of a problem, the delineation of it for research purposes, and the design of the research plan. The project seminar may also encourage the formation of small groups to work on the same or similar studies.

Through the project seminar the student comes into contact with a variety of research proposals and plans. A student presenting his subject for research or his plan has the experience of clarifying it for the group and defending it or modifying it in the light of the group's criticism. The group has the opportunity to apply critical thinking to research.

In a few schools the seminar is a continuing body to which the student reports progress throughout his research; in most, however, the seminar only functions during the initial stages after which the student becomes responsible to his particular advisor or advisors. The learning situations even vary in the latter plan. For example, in one school the project seminar meets for only one session, while in another, eight meetings are scheduled, and the student has the experience of reading a completed project, preparing an abstract, and reviewing research methodology. In a school maintaining the seminar over the year, students engaged in individual projects keep a research diary of the work done on their projects and report on their activities.

Several trends may be noted in regard to the project seminar. In schools where the research methods course and the project are concurrent, the research course frequently fulfills the function of the seminar. As mentioned above, where the large group project under faculty leadership is undertaken there is no need for a special project seminar. In a few schools, however, the seminar form has taken on greater significance, and the project or a paper in lieu of it is the student contribution to a seminar of definite content.

THE PROJECT

The most rigorous and lengthy learning experience of the research sequence is the master's project. While the master's project is not necessarily part of the research sequence, the major responsibility for planning and supervising projects, in most schools, falls upon the research faculty. The trend toward the large group project also has made for the greater integration of the project with the research sequence. However, changes in the nature of the project requirement, and efforts to integrate the project with other components of the curriculum may result in shifting the place of the project in the total curriculum.

The project is a second year learning experience for social work students, and in most schools the student engages in project work throughout the second year. In several schools this period is short-ened to the last two quarters or the last semester of the second year. In one school, however, the project is completed before the last quarter, and in another the student finishes his project in the summer following his regular academic program. The amount of time devoted to the project and the place of the project in the total academic calendar have raised problems for the schools. Comple-tion of the project at the same time as the student is bringing to a close other major learning experiences may make demands beyond the learning capacity of the student.

In most schools students have the choice of individual or group projects. However, there has been a growing tendency for projects to be of a group nature, and the individual project may become a relatively rare experience in the near future.[3] Recently one school has dropped the research project requirement and has substituted an intensive library investigation of some methodological problem in social work research. Other schools are also experimenting with seminar plans in which the focus is analysis of published material rather than original investigation. In a few schools the student may substitute a paper for the project requirement, but receives less or no point credit toward his degree.

Much consideration has been given to the relative merits of the individual and group projects as learning experiences. Generaliza-tions are difficult to make because of the variations in each type of learning situation. However, issues frequently raised when com-paring the two approaches are summarized below:

*Value of the Individual Project*

1. The student can gain the full learning experience of problem-solving in research only if he undertakes an independent ex-ploration in which he is responsible for the whole of the process from problem identification to completion of the re-port.
2. The differing abilities and work tempos of the students make it difficult if not impossible for all to participate fully in com-mon research.
3. The individual project permits the student to be totally in-

3 Report of the Biestek Committee, 9.

volved in the research itself without the complication and time loss of group participation.

4. Where students are involved in individual projects, each has the advantage of contact with a large variety of on-going pieces of research.

5. The individual project makes more feasible the evaluation of each student's work.

*Value of the Group Project*

1. The student has the experience of participating in research as a cooperative activity which resembles the situation he will face when in practice.

2. The student enjoys the advantage of group stimulation.

3. The student is able to participate in a piece of research of larger significance.

4. There is less opportunity for individual bias as the students are constantly interacting in an atmosphere of critical thinking.

5. The group provides a sound situation for learning principles and methods of research.

6. The group project provides more opportunity for all students to participate in a uniformly acceptable learning experience through controls exercised by the faculty.

7. Where available time is limited as it is in the master's program, the learning experiences of the students may be adapted to their capacity and may be regulated to emphasize those aspects of research which the faculty believes most important for the students' education. Thus, the project becomes integrated with the other educational objectives of the curriculum.

8. The student finds satisfaction in the group experience and develops a more favorable attitude toward research, particularly since the group project is usually completed within the normal time allowed.

The project experience, whether individual or group, has been criticized by those favoring its modification on the grounds that neither the time available nor the students' ability in research makes the empirical research project a fruitful learning experience. The project has also been considered to make unrealistic demands on the students' energies in view of the total educational expectations of the master's curriculum. Library research, on the other hand, has been described by those employing this approach as a more appropriate way of developing research attitudes and knowledge in practitioners of methods other than research.

Although the terms individual and group project have been used broadly, there are many variations in the way schools approach both types of projects. The number of students, and their organization, in group projects differ widely. The group project may be merely a cooperative research of two or at most a very limited number of students. These small groups may function as a unit or may have a relatively loose structure. For example, in one school the students engage in "cluster studies;" two or more students working either together or separately approach the same question from different points of view or examine different groups in relation to the same problem.

On the other hand, research problems selected by the faculty for formal group projects may involve as many as 30 or 40 students. The experience of one school indicates that from 10 to 15 constitutes the optimum group. Another school has found that in simpler kinds of projects as many as 25 may be an effective working group whereas in more complex projects, 15 to 18 are preferable. In both schools there is direct faculty supervision as well as some latitude for student initiative in planning the research. However, the school suggesting the smaller group relies more heavily on student administration of the project.

The elements of learning experience provided by the project, whether individual or group, depend to some extent on the manner in which the learning situation of the project is structured by the school. Although there are no sharp distinctions in the plans of schools for the project, learning situations are basically of three types:

1. The students have responsibility for the whole of the project from problem selection to writing of the report. Some schools encourage students, in both individual and group projects, to select their

own topics and to undertake independently the whole of the research. However, even in schools with such a policy, the students frequently rely on suggestions from faculty, field advisors, staff of field agency, or proposals of other agencies.

2. Research problems are provided for the student, but the remainder of the research is undertaken entirely by the students. In both individual and group projects, the school may arrange for research topics with the agency in which the students are placed. Where group projects are formally organized under faculty supervision, the problem is selected in advance although some freedom may be left the students in delineating it for research purposes. In programs of this type, the amount of faculty participation varies, and the faculty may take major responsibility for certain phases of the research.

3. Faculty assumes responsibility for problem selection and formulation, design of the research, and administration of the project. The students in this type of program participate in a study arranged for, planned, and administered by the faculty. Usually the project is a study or part of a study in which a member of the faculty is particularly interested. While the students are generally oriented to the whole of the research, they participate most directly in the collection and analysis of data, conclusion drawing and report writing. Even these aspects may be carried out under close faculty direction.

The three types of project plans noted above indicate methods of dividing responsibility for the elements of the project experience between faculty and students. One of the basic educational problems of the project is planning for division of labor which will at the same time provide a sound learning experience for the students participating. Among the reasons which have made the group project acceptable to many schools has been its potentiality for more effective use of both student and faculty time and effort within the limits of the crowded social work curriculum.

Three aspects of division of responsibility particularly affecting the learning experience of the group project have been: administration of the project, the research tasks of the students, and the writing of the research report.

In smaller group projects, administration may be an informal arrangement among the students who decide on their own allocation of responsibility. Where student administration has functioned in larger projects, the faculty has generally suggested the plan for a definite structure, and committees have frequently been used to organize and coordinate various aspects of the project. In many larger projects which are faculty sponsored the faculty assumes almost complete responsibility for administering the research.

In nearly all instances, responsibility for various parts of the research itself is divided among the students. However, some phases of the research, such as data collecting or analysis, may be participated in by all students. In one program, after the data are collected and organized by the total group, each student is provided with a mimeographed summary and undertakes his own analysis and report on the total data. In another plan, each student is responsible for the analysis of a certain portion of the data. In still other programs or parts of those cited above, only a small group or committee participates in particular activities, such as pre-testing the schedule, editing the data, or collecting the bibliography. Various procedures are employed for the students reporting on the project. In some programs each student is responsible for a written report on the whole of the project. In others, the student may only write a particular chapter or section. In some cases, part of the report is a joint undertaking, and part is contributed individually. Finally, the whole report may be a joint undertaking although each student may be required to organize a complete draft.

## SUGGESTED LEARNING EXPERIENCES IN RELATION TO DESIRABLE EDUCATIONAL OBJECTIVES

A limited number of types of learning experiences are analyzed below with regard to their significance for the objectives suggested by this project as desirable for the research curriculum. The learning experiences selected for analysis are those peculiar to the research objectives; more general experiences common to all areas of the curriculum, such as reading and discussion, are not included. It should be noted that neither the learning experiences presently provided in schools nor those considered below are necessarily

indicative of all the possibilities for learning experiences in this field. One of the difficulties in achieving the objectives of the research sequence undoubtedly has been the paucity of experimentation in learning experiences.

It should be noted, too, that the learning experiences suggested are essentially those currently employed. The primary purpose of this analysis is to relate these learning experiences to the objectives distinguished in the first part of this report. Thus, the major concern here is the adaptation of these learning experiences to the objectives for the research sequence. The learning experiences are not presented as models, but rather as illustrations of integrating learning experiences with sequence goals. Learning experiences, like any other tool, may be applied in a variety of ways, and their ultimate value can be gauged only by how well they satisfy particular needs and teaching techniques in achieving the results desired.

The learning experiences examined below are those which seek to support more than one major objective of the research sequence. This type of learning experience has the advantage of being economical in a sequence which has relatively limited time for realizing several objectives and where the concentration is not so much on specific knowledge or skills as on the development of broader attitudes and capacities toward research and problem-solving. Further, it is more likely that the student preparing to be a practitioner in other than the research method, will obtain satisfaction from, and consequently be motivated by, learning experiences which have greater breadth. More specific objectives take on meaning from their relationship to the whole.

ANALYSIS OF RESEARCH STUDIES

Analysis of research studies as a learning experience has the potentiality of supporting the objectives suggested in the areas of scientific method, research in social work, problem-solving through the research method, and statistics. As a learning experience, analysis of research studies has the important advantage of student participation in an activity directly related to his future professional behavior. Research studies should be introduced with appropriate concern for student motivation and readiness, and should be or-

ganized to provide a sequential experience to deepen and broaden the student's interest and ability not only in reading research, but also in the other capacities which this learning experience supports.

The case method developed in the physical sciences may not be totally applicable to either social science or social work research, but it does present an approach which can be adapted to their needs. The structuring of research learning around studies focusing on such core professional problems as measurement of need and services or evaluation of effectiveness of service may be considered roughly analogous to the development of concepts or principles which serve as the core of the case method in teaching the physical sciences. Though the use of social work studies may be illustrative more of refining an art than advancing a science, many of the same factors emphasized in the science case method are pertinent, *e.g.*, technical difficulties in the problem, historical background of the development of the problem, setting of the problem in the specialized field and in the general social framework, and human aspects affecting the solution of the problem.[4]

While the formal organization of historical cases has the possibility of clearly incorporating materials pertinent to the desired objectives, some of these benefits may be obtained through an organized approach to the examination of a set of separate studies, which focus on a particular issue or problem. There is definite need, however, for the development of historical materials in the field of social work research to supply the background for analysis of current studies and trends.[5] Through this type of contact the student has the opportunity to gain perspective both on the growth of social work knowledge and on the factors influencing the nature of this growth. The integrated use of research documents involves the student in the profession's scientific problem-solving efforts and permits him to participate in the continuous

4 See Leonard K. Nash, "The Use of Historical Cases in Science Teaching" in *General Education in Science, op. cit.,* 97–118.
5 A valuable contribution in this direction has been made by Sidney E. Zimbalist, "Major Trends in Social Work Research" (unpublished doctoral dissertation, George Warren Brown School of Social Work, Washington University, St. Louis, 1955). Zimbalist analyzes the following trends: "The Search for Causes," "The Determination of Financial Needs: Standard Budgets," "The Rise and Decline of the Social Survey Movement," "The Struggle for Uniform Statistics," "Index-making in Social Work," "The Study of Social Work Effectiveness."

adventure of problem-solving which is fundamental to the development of knowledge in any field.

The analysis of studies should not, however, be limited to formal research reports. In addition, critical attention should be given to contributions to the field which are not usually considered research by research standards, but which are quantitatively far more abundant in social work literature and with which the student is likely to have greater contact. The student also needs some experience in evaluating research reported in digests and summaries. While one of the problems of research teaching is that studies are frequently not fully reported, the practitioner will often be in the position of relying on even less extensive reports in the literature of the field. In some cases research reports themselves may be too technically oriented for practitioner consumption, and simplified digests may serve a constructive purpose. However, the student must be able to approach these sources with some critical skill if he is to be an intelligent consumer.[6]

PROJECTS

One of the major issues in regard to the project, whether individual or group, is the relationship of the project to the objectives defined in the research sequence. Because of the many problems encountered with projects as learning experiences, undue emphasis may easily be placed upon successful completion of the project rather than on the objectives to be fulfilled through it. This is not to deny the importance of structuring the project so that the student obtains the positive satisfaction of successful problem-solving which strengthens his own confidence and encourages him to embark on even more complex tasks. However, though completion is an important goal in learning experiences, there are other elements necessary if the completion is fully to represent the objectives desired.

It may be helpful to view the project not as a unit but as a series of learning experiences supporting several objectives. Thus in examining any particular approach to the project, it is important

[6] For a discussion of teaching approaches to this type of material, see American Council on Education, *Science Reasoning and Understanding* (Dubuque, Iowa: William C. Brown, 1954), particularly chapters III–IX.

to be aware of the kinds of learning experiences provided and the objectives which may be achieved through these experiences. Is appropriate emphasis given to those learning experiences which are considered essential for the research objectives planned for practitioners of service methods? In some projects, as noted above, the breadth of the research experience becomes telescoped, and the learning experiences most important for the student are modified in the process. Often in order to move the project into the more active stages commencing with data collecting, the major responsibility for the early and extensive exploration resulting in the formulation of a fruitful hypothesis or significant study question is carried by faculty leadership. However, it is these aspects of problem-solving which are particularly significant as learning experiences for the practitioner. For as Gordon states, "The knowledge of technique applicable only to the later stages of the [research] process leaves him [the student] ill equipped to effectively relate research to the problems of practice since they offer little help to him in determining what needs to be known and how to look for it." [7] The kind of research problem-solving in which the practitioner most often engages and to which research training has much to contribute is the selecting, organizing, and examining of information pertinent to the solution of a problem. Emphasis on the techniques and procedures of data collecting is more valuable as a learning experience for the role of research practitioner than for the typical practitioner of a service method.

As Charlotte Towle and others have remarked, the literature of social casework (and her comment might be extended to the literature of social work generally) is not "cumulative and structured." [8] This failure to develop an organized background of knowledge frequently leads to isolated problem-solving in social work practice. Research, on the other hand, if it is meaningful, seeks to broaden the area of scientific knowledge through systematic exploration and expansion of the already developed knowledge base. The beginning exploration of the problem requires the student to

[7] William E. Gordon, *Toward Basic Research in Social Work* (St. Louis: George Warren Brown School of Social Work, Washington University, 1951), 11.
[8] Towle, *op. cit.*, 278; Roger W. Little, "The Literature of Social Casework," *Social Casework*, XXXIII (July, 1952), 287–91.

relate his problem to the efforts of others in his own and related fields who have grappled with similar problems. The experience of selecting information pertinent to the solution of the problem involves not only systematizing information, but also knowledge of sources of information and their reliability, ability to select adequate and reliable samples of information, and ability to evaluate the information for relevance and bias.

This element of problem-solving demands most of the critical thinking abilities present in problem-solving generally. If one of the general objectives of social work education is to help students become more theory-minded and more aware of the possibilities of generalization, this will not be achieved by a research experience which avoids or lessens emphasis on the aspect of research which is founded on the knowledge base of the profession.

Other features of the project which require consideration relate to the degree to which the project fosters the integration of the research experience with other aspects of the student's total learning. Some approaches to the project have tended to weaken the contact between research and the rest of faculty or between research and the student's field experience.[9] While for administrative purposes it is no doubt simpler to place the project more closely under the aegis of the school and the research faculty, this removal from the service methods sequence and the field practice agency raises questions as to the assumption that research is a normal function of the agency and an integral part of the practitioner's role. If these assumptions are incorrect, there appears little reason for instructing the practitioner in a methodology which he is unlikely to use. If they are correct, then the school must provide a learning experience which links the agency and the practitioner's role with research.[10]

The problem in regard to the project is one of placing it in its proper proportions within the curriculum and emphasizing those aspects of it as a learning experience which are most important and

9 The tendency of research teaching to be too "colored" by "professional research thinking and methods" was remarked upon at the 1948 AASSW Conference meeting. See unpublished minutes of discussion of session #17.
10 "Workshop B, Research in Social Agencies—Implications for the Teaching of Social Work Students," *Social Work Research*, Subject Area Workshop Report, 1954 *Proceedings* (New York: Council on Social Work Education, 1954), 11.

meaningful to the student. The objectives supported by the learning experience of the project must be realistically evaluated, and the project may need to be viewed as a selective rather than a general learning experience.

For example, the student with more interest and ability in research, who is preparing for the role of research practitioner and who may later seek further training as a research specialist, may find an intensive project experience of value. For other students the project may be one among a variety of possible learning experiences. Briefer and more limited laboratory contacts with an ongoing piece of research may be developed as part of the research methods course. While an intensive analysis of a problem in social work may be a valuable learning experience, other means than the present project method exist for achieving this. Seminar approaches are being attempted in some schools. Another alternative might be a thorough development of the early stages of a problem in practice up to the point of testing the solutions or exploring the questions raised. This would be followed by a brief experience in data collection and analysis with again greater emphasis on possible conclusions and their implications. Such a paper might be linked both to the student's methods faculty and his field work placement. The student would have the learning experience of delineating a problem, exploring and evaluating what is already known, suggesting alternative solutions, recognizing the role of research methods, drawing conclusions, and considering their implications for practice.

Obviously one of the issues in planning learning experiences is whether the objectives for the practitioner of methods other than research may be fulfilled by a practical research experience emphasizing specific elements of the total research process. Several experienced teachers in the field have raised serious questions about the validity of any approach which does not give the student an opportunity to be involved in research which does not encompass all phases of the process. Alternative approaches are here advanced not with the purpose of differing with this assumption, but rather with the purpose of structuring the most adequate learning experience within the present curriculum limits. In view of these limits, is it not better to stress those phases of research most important for practitioners generally? Since many learning experiences in practical research result in providing either a somewhat superficial approach to all aspects or a concentrated experience in a few, is it possible to design a research learning experience which places greatest emphasis on those facets most valuable to future "service" practitioners?

RESEARCH DESIGNS AND CLASS RESEARCH PROJECTS
(research project done in the research class)

The designing of a research project is frequently undertaken as either a class effort or an individual student assignment. In a few instances, in addition to the research design, the class participates as a group in the completion of a small research study. As a learning experience the preparation of a research design provides an opportunity for meeting many of the basic objectives of the research sequence. Ideally, as in the project, the student: (1) participates in problem-solving with emphasis on the research method; (2) follows the principles of the scientist; (3) is made aware of the field of research in social work, its function and relationship to practice; and (4) plans in quantitative terms. The limitations of the design are that the student does not have the experience of testing the adequacy of his plan in the completion of the research. However, if the learning situation includes the student's defense of his design, preferably in class, many of the factors influencing the conclusion of the research may be brought into focus. The use of the same or a limited number of research problems for the class and the presentation and examination of a variety of approaches to the same problem tend to lessen the laboratory sterility of the experience and heighten the students' awareness of the artfulness of research problem-solving. The selection of the research problem by the instructor also limits the students' designs to areas productive for learning experience.

The development of a research project in which the whole class participates has the value of providing a learning experience in the total process of research problem-solving under faculty guidance. In most schools, the amount of time allocated to the course aspects of the research sequence does not permit this type of learning situation. However, as has been suggested above, the large group project is in reality very similiar to a class project. If the research sequence is considered as a combination of one semester of introductory content and two semesters of laboratory or practical experience in research, the heavy weighting given the latter aspect (for students not specializing in research) raises serious question as to the appropriateness of the investment in this learning experience. A possible solution, in view of the time consuming nature of the present project system and its unbalanced relationship to the total sequence, is the development of modest class projects whose goal would be not the fulfillment of any formal requirement but rather a learning experience in research problem-solving. The class project could then be made an integral part of research methods courses, coordinated with other content, and allocated time in terms of the total plan of learning experiences. The emphasis here would be clearly on the learning situation uncomplicated by other goals which frequently result in the present project approach serving several purposes inadequately.

As mentioned earlier, the kinds of learning experiences suggested for the research sequence are those which stress the inter-relationship of the objectives of the sequence rather than those which support specific objectives as discrete elements. Mastery of many specific techniques, while no doubt valuable for themselves as well as pertinent to basic principles and methods, is not a learning experience sufficiently meaningful for the student preparing to be a social work practitioner. It is difficult to plan a research sequence when students have little background in the fundamentals of research or statistics without attempting to make up for these deficiencies. It is necessary, however, to develop learning experiences which will recognize these deficiencies and despite them, still concentrate on the objectives of the sequence.

This is especially pertinent when the goals of the sequence are directed toward *understanding* rather than *doing* research.

# CHAPTER IV

# Organization of Learning Experiences[1]

## CONTINUITY AND SEQUENCE

Continuity and sequence of learning experience are dependent on the identification of major curriculum elements, their reiteration, and their progressive development. In the research component continuity and sequence are at present largely a product of the relationship between the introductory methods course or courses and the project. The trend toward viewing the project as a learning experience rather than a test of student ability in research, and the incorporation of the project as a unit in the research sequence rather than its being a discrete entity, make possible an effective learning organization.

Generally speaking, the potentialities for both continuity and sequence within the research component appear greater when there is a temporal sequence between the methods course and the project than when the two are concurrent experiences. The former situation allows for "successive experience" building toward more extensive and intensive capacities, while the latter concentrates the whole of the learning experience within a more limited span. On the other hand, if the major research curriculum elements are identified and integrated within the rest of the curriculum, it is possible for the continuity and sequence of these elements to be achieved through the relationship between the research component and the other components of the curriculum.

The timing of the introductory methods course is important not only as it affects the research sequence, but also in relation to integration with other elements of the curriculum. In present curriculum planning, there is an evident desire to maintain a close link between the research methods course and the project. This has resulted in the research course being given, in most instances, at the end of the first year or the beginning of the second year. If, however, the research methods course, as presently appears to be

1 See Tyler, *op. cit.*, 54–7, for the frame of reference of this analysis.

the case, carries major responsibility for important elements of the total curriculum, these should be introduced as early as possible in the student's learning experience, with the whole of the curriculum, including the remainder of the research sequence, providing an opportunity for broadening and deepening these elements. There would thus seem advantages for continuity and sequence not available in many present approaches. Such a plan, too, would more clearly relate the project and the research methods course as complementary experiences, rather than making the latter, as sometimes occurs, serve mainly as preparatory training for the former.

Aside from these considerations, there are other problems affecting continuity and sequence which are related to clarification of curriculum objectives of the research component. For example, while critical thinking about research contributions is considered one of the major objectives of the research sequence, the student frequently does not have sufficient opportunity to exercise and develop this skill within the research sequence. Critical analysis of research studies is usually undertaken in the introductory course, often before the student has had sufficient professional knowledge to deal with their content. These studies are usually of much greater complexity than the problems the student will face in his own project at a later point in his learning experience.[2] Unless other courses in the curriculum strengthen this objective, the students' reading of and critical thinking about research contributions will be limited to the introductory research course. The organization of many project programs either leaves little time for, or dispenses entirely with, the students' critical analysis of the pertinent literature of social work and related fields. In some instances, the students' direct participation occurs after this step in the research process; in others, the pressure toward completion makes for least attention to be given the exploration and evaluation of previous efforts to solve the problem or closely related problems.

[2] While the student is not expected to participate in research of equal complexity to that read and analyzed, the introduction of the project experience after such reading does not provide a learning experience of appropriate sequence unless the student has opportunity for further development of the ability to read and evaluate research studies.

Similar questions may be raised about the degree to which the research sequence provides for continuity and development of such objectives as knowledge of the function of research, or the ability for scientifically oriented problem-solving. The general issue is the extent of support given the major curriculum objectives of the research component through continuity and sequence of its learning experiences. Are the learning experiences of the research sequence scattered among many objectives rather than concentrated on the major ones? Does the student obtain a superficial acquaintance with a variety of content which dissolves rather than crystallizes the goals desired? Does the sequence of learning experiences result in development of capacities in conformity with curriculum objectives, or does it effect an imbalance between primary and secondary objectives?

## INTEGRATION

Integration, or the development of a "unified view" of the objectives of the research curriculum, is achieved in two ways: (1) the inclusion of other elements of the curriculum within the research sequence, and (2) the penetration of research objectives into the learning experiences provided by other elements of the curriculum.

*Inclusion of other elements of the curriculum within the research sequence.*

The major opportunity for integration of other elements of the curriculum into the research sequence occurs in the project program. Faculty members, other than research and field work personnel, have roles at several points in current project planning. The selection of project problems is frequently participated in by the field agency, field faculty, faculty of the practice method concerned as well as the research faculty. Where group or individual projects are dependent on agency material, some relationship is generally established between the school and the agency. In several schools, these contacts are made in advance, and the project topics are the result of joint consultation rather than merely formal clearance with the agency. In one school, selection of topics is done by an advisory committee on research consisting of agency and school representatives. Another school relies on the agency and field instructor to suggest and formulate problems for students in placement. In some instances, agencies are encouraged to propose on their own initiative researchable topics for student projects.

The faculty as a whole or a committee of the faculty has the responsibility for selecting and approving topics for student research in some schools. The large group projects involving so great a proportion of the student body have made these projects of concern to the total faculty. In some programs, selection of projects occurs through consultation between the research department and the director of the major methods sequence involved. In individual projects the faculty advisor often helps the student in the selection of problems for the project. In one school, a standing committee of the faculty assists the advisor in this function. In some programs, agency personnel participate beyond the selection of the project topic; they may help in the initial planning stages and give intermittent consultation. More intensive agency participation at times occurs when the student's placement is too remote for convenient contact with the research faculty. In such situations the field work and methods faculty in touch with the agency may also assume greater responsibility. In one experimental program, students were attached to a research project totally under the aegis of a field work agency. The agency research program was under the leadership of a worker responsible solely for the research.[3] Other schools have also attempted to bring their own research personnel into close collaboration with the agency where student research is undertaken. Research thus tends to become part of the student's normal field work responsibility. One school follows the practice of having a member of the agency staff attend supervisory conferences on the project. However, the policy of another school, where the agency and field instructor cooperate in suggesting topics for research, is to avoid further agency re-

[3] Jean M. Arsenian, "Toward a Research Training Program in Psychiatric Social Work," reprinted from *Journal of Psychiatric Social Work* (October 1954), 42–6.

sponsibility because of the possibilities for confusion and loss of time to agency personnel and faculty in indiscriminate consultation.

The growth of the large group project plan has frequently lessened the amount of direct contact of the faculty as a whole with student research, although it is possible for student projects to be led by faculty members other than the research faculty. In the group project faculty members may serve on the project committee or act as consultants, but responsibility tends to be focused in the project director. In the individual or small group project the students may be assigned to any member of the faculty throughout the research or after the initial stages. In an effort to continue within the group project this role of the faculty, one school arranged for students to be assigned to advisors after data collection. Each student was given an individual task of analyzing, drawing conclusions, and reporting in regard to a particular aspect of the data, and the faculty advisor's role was to assist the student in effectively carrying out this responsibility.[4] Other plans to integrate the faculty as a whole in research include having the leadership of the project seminar shared between a member of the research faculty and one from another method, and arranging a faculty seminar for discussion of student projects.

*The penetration of research objectives into other elements of the curriculum.*

It is difficult to gauge the extent to which objectives of the research sequence are shared with other components of the curriculum. Examination of course materials shows, on the whole, only a limited presence of these objectives, but they may be present without being explicitly indicated.

The brief summary below is, therefore, not presented as representative of current teaching, but rather as indicative of some of the problems and approaches suggested by course outlines and field manuals.

---

[4] *Summary of Research 1955–1956* (George Warren Brown School of Social Work, Washington University, St. Louis, 1956), 13–26.

*Systematic problem-solving:*   This objective is emphasized in many areas of the curriculum. In some, such as casework methods, all or nearly all of the basic elements in problem-solving and their interrelationship are defined, and the student is expected to develop skill in their use. Ability in systematic problem-solving is also stressed, though to a lesser extent, in casework field manuals. Other segments of the curriculum tend to emphasize particular aspects of problem-solving. Some require the student to become familiar with sources of information important for problem-solving, and in addition may expect him to be able to make some evaluation or appraisal of the use of these sources.

*Principles of scientific inquiry:*   The principles or generally accepted assumptions of scientific inquiry, such as causality, tentativeness, consistency, objectivity, and so on, are rarely found related to course content. In one course in human growth and behavior, assumptions underlying the scientific study of man are established as the introductory base for the course content. Specific reference is made to the relationship of abstraction and partialization in theory and the emphasis on uniqueness and unity (one of the major difficulties of the practitioner relating to research). Generally speaking, the identification of concepts and their application in problem-solving does not appear to be a frequent objective of social work courses although the use of "basic concepts and schemes of viewing the particular phenomenon" is important in providing a structure for scientifically oriented problem-solving.[5]

One approach to teaching the nature of scientific inquiry goes beyond the identification of relevant concepts and treats with their historical development. The development of concepts, including the factors that have influenced their formation, is a valuable learning experience for the student being oriented to the scientific "folkways" of his profession.[6] Through it, he participates in the process of scientific inquiry and follows the

[5] Tyler, *op. cit.*, 46. The use of the term "basic concepts" in social work to refer to such professional practices as confidentiality and democratic choice of client has frequently led to their confusion with scientific concepts.
[6] See Leonard K. Nash, *op. cit.*, 97–118.

development of knowledge in the continuous pattern of problem-solving. The student may learn to recognize the principles most conducive to the growth of a professional knowledge base. The lack of attention in the classroom to the role of generalization in problem-solving is also reflected in field work objectives. Rarely is mention made in field work manuals of the ability to relate theory and practice as one of the goals of the student's practice experience.

*Attitude of critical thinking:* Though behavior involving the process and principles of problem-solving may not be one of the major elements of learning experience, it may be assumed that an attitude of critical thinking is a widespread objective even though no specific reference is made to it. However, if this is true for classroom learning, few schools view it as sufficiently important to include it as one of the objectives of field work experience. One of the schools maintaining this objective expects of its student field supervisors, "respect for student's ideas and willingness to let him experiment, within agency policy and setting." This school questions whether "we tend to be over-cautious, or too fearful of damage to agency or client or group." The importance of an attitude of critical thinking cannot be overestimated. Without a sense of freedom in inquiry and experimentation, the practice of problem-solving may become a sterile exercise in the application of a dogmatic system.

*The value of research knowledge to practice:* Courses in community organization and administration, particularly, point up the kinds of fact-finding studies necessary if the function of community organization or administration is to be effectively performed. Courses in other fields appear to give less weight to this objective although the plan of one casework course has included not only the contribution of research, but also areas needing research as well as the problems and obstacles in undertaking research in casework. The actual incorporation of research findings and the demonstration of their relevance to practice, however, does not frequently appear as one of the learning experiences stressed in the social work curriculum.

*The role of the practitioner in research:* This objective is given consideration in some methods courses. For example, in one group work course distinction is made between the independent research responsibilities of the practitioner and his function in relation to the research specialist. The field manual of another school includes the objective of understanding the use of recording for research purposes. A casework course has content on the use of casework skills in research. Courses and field manuals in medical and psychiatric social work emphasize the role of the social worker in interdisciplinary research. The greater emphasis in these fields on the role of the practitioner in research is probably a response to the social worker's functioning in an environment of other professions which apply scientific method and employ research procedures. A medical social work field manual, for example, points to research as one of the common methods linking all professions in the setting.

*Relationship of practice knowledge to research:* Somewhat different from the role of the practitioner and his skills in research undertakings is the objective of the practitioner being aware of the interplay between practice knowledge and research. This objective is rarely alluded to directly in course materials. An illustration of this objective is the suggestion made in one casework course that the completion of the casework process may be in a research evaluation or follow-up of the casework service.

*Responsibility of social agencies for research:* The responsibility of social agencies for research has been found both in courses on administration and community organization and in field work manuals. The manual of one school states, for example, that "recognition" by the agency and supervisor of the value of research is important for the student's learning experience. Another manual states that relationship of agencies to community need has as one of its normal concomitants recognition of the place of research.

*Relationship of social work to knowledge in the social sciences and related fields:* It is difficult to judge to what extent social science materials are introduced in social work courses. In some schools a special course may be given relating social science content to the practice of social work.[7] In others, though not fre-

---

[7] Herman D. Stein, "Social Science in Social Work Practice and Education," *Social Casework*, XXXVI (April 1955).

quently, social science knowledge, where relevant, is directly related to the course material. In addition to the above curriculum elements, a number of schools further the general objective of disciplined thought and performance by adhering in all courses to a uniform manual of style encompassing the principles of scholarly writing.

As noted earlier, the observations made in this section are based on a review of curriculum materials. Other elements related to the research sequence may be present, though they have not been delineated in these materials. However, in general it would appear that the social work curriculum demonstrates very limited integration of the objectives of the research sequence.

The failure to integrate the other aspects of the curriculum with the research sequence has resulted in overloading the research sequence and giving it responsibility for elements of curriculum which might be dealt with more satisfactorily in other places. Failure to integrate has also prevented the research sequence from clearly delineating its objectives and organizing its learning experiences. The research sequence has often been viewed as the catch-all for the "scientific" in the social work curriculum. This approach has fostered the dichotomy between the "scientific" and the "practical" in social work training. The student's professional identification with the components of the curriculum supporting the latter has effectively decreased his respect for the contribution of the research component and consequently his respect for any effort to provide a more scientific base for practice. Thus the present lack of integration of research objectives with the rest of the curriculum affects the goals of the total curriculum.

## CONCLUSIONS REGARDING LEARNING EXPERIENCES

The foregoing analysis of learning experiences indicates several significant issues in curriculum planning for the research sequence:

1. Clarification of curriculum objectives.
2. Development of learning experiences within the research component which support these objectives.
3. Organization of the research component so that continuity and sequence of learning experiences within the sequence and their integration with other components of the curriculum most effectively achieve the major objectives desired.
4. Appropriate division of responsibility for objectives between the research and other components of the curriculum, as well as between the undergraduate and graduate levels.

The learning experiences currently provided by the research curricula of schools of social work tend to reflect a conflict of objectives between enabling the practitioner to accomplish his own professional roles more effectively and preparing the practitioner for some level of skill in the research method as an end in itself. Although most schools state they are not preparing practitioners for doing research (and the few that express this goal expect only modest and limited competence), the core of the research sequence is generally the research project. The timing and content of the introductory methods course, often supplemented by the project seminar, are arranged with a view toward maximum efficiency in project production. The project itself requires the heaviest investment of the student's time and energy among the learning experiences of the research sequence.

As suggested earlier, if the research sequence were less focused on the project, the planning of the research sequence could be more related to the appropriateness of introducing elements of the research sequence in relation to the total curriculum. For example, it would be of value to arrange an early introduction to the field of research in social work, the scientific approach to problem-solving, the tactics and strategy of research, and the analysis of social statistics. More intensive critical reading of social work research would depend not only on the foundation provided in the introductory research course, but also on some experience with social work content and problem-solving in relation to it. Emphasis on critical reading of contemporary research as well as examination of trends and problems in social work research might well come toward the end of the student's professional training. The assumption here is, of course, that the other components of the curriculum will provide the continuity of learning experiences necessary to the organization of the research sequence. Although the ability to read and critically to evaluate research contributions is one of the major goals of the research sequence, the student has relatively little opportunity to practice this kind of behavior in the research and other components of the curriculum. Studies should be introduced in both research and other courses to provide an orderly sequence of learning experience for the student.

Finally, many of the objectives of the research component require reinforcement by, or incorporation within, other components of the curriculum. While the elements, principles, and attitudes toward scientific problem-solving may be delineated within the research sequence, their relationship to the student's future professional behavior is basically dependent on learning situations in class and field practice which prepare him for his primary professional role. Neither from the point of view of content nor of learning principles can the research sequence do the job alone.[8]

The scientific method of problem-solving is not a static or fixed entity which may be transferred directly from the context of research to that of practice. While certain common sense generalizations may be constant, each field must develop its own approaches to problem-solving. Even if there were much that was transferable from the research method to the practice methods, from the point of view of learning experience it would be preferable, where possible, to have the student's learning directly related to situations in his own practice. The student has greater motivation in these situations; he has opportunity to carry out the behavior in relation to the content for which the objective has been planned; he is more likely to achieve success and to obtain greater satisfaction from success; finally, he is in a better position to appraise his own

[8] There appears to be some difference of opinion in education circles as to the transferability of training to think critically. Edward M. Glaser, after surveying the studies concerning training to think critically and transfer of training to think critically, stated, "All point to the conclusion that the content alone of any subject is not likely to give general training to the mind, and is not likely to develop a generalized ability to think critically." Edward M. Glaser, *An Experiment in the Development of Critical Thinking* (New York: Teachers College, Columbia University, 1941), 8. Also see Dressel and Mayhew, *op. cit.*, 175–6.

standards in such situations than in the application of critical thinking to content in which he has least competence.

It is not so much a question of integrating or permeating the other components of the curriculum as of having them assume their appropriate responsibility for some of the objectives of the research component. Emphasis in the courses on methods and social policy, on problem-solving, generalization and conceptualization, the use of relevant knowledge from other fields such as the social sciences, the application of research findings, the location and use of social statistics would not only provide sound learning experiences, but would also make it possible for the research sequence to structure more appropriate objectives and provide more adequate learning experiences for their achievement. The analysis of the integration of research objectives in the curriculum, in the preceding section, has shown that, while some attempts at integration have been made, it is certainly not a widespread practice either in the classroom or in the field. Finally there is need for the schools to develop some general expectations of undergraduate education in regard to the research component. Such knowledge as basic statistics and logic and the scientific method should be among the undergraduate foundations of professional education. Not only is the professional curriculum too full to include such content, but the undergraduate period is a more natural point in the student's education for him to acquire such knowledge. It may very well be, in educational needs as in emotional needs, that gaps in the appropriate sequence can never be really successfully compensated for later.

# Appendix

**Goals of the Research Sequence Indicated by Schools of Social Work for Practitioners of Methods other than Social Work Research ***

| Goals of Research Sequence | Number of Schools |
|---|---|
| 1. Practitioner's own practice | |
| Attitude of critical thinking | 11 |
| Ability to apply scientific approach to problem-solving in practice | 13 |
| 2. Theory and method of practitioner | |
| Attitude of critical thinking | 3 |
| 3. The field of social work research | |
| Acquaintance with nature of research | 11 |
| Appreciation of research as an approach for extending social work knowledge | 11 |
| 4. Knowledge arising from research | |
| Ability to evaluate critically | 17 |
| Ability to interpret and use pertinent research findings in practice | 11 |
| 5. The practice of research | |
| Attitude of responsibility toward contributing to the advancement of professional knowledge | 7 |
| Ability to participate in research activities | 16 |
| Ability to undertake research independently | 3 |
| 6. Other professional responsibilities | |
| Ability to communicate clearly about the field of social work | 2 |
| Ability to study and analyze social welfare programs and problems | 4 |

* Based on goals *specified* in school catalogs, course outlines and materials, research project manuals, survey of the Biestek Committee, published and unpublished reports of research faculty, and other curriculum data.

TABLE II

**Types of Research Functions Performed by, or Expected of, Social Work Practitioners, According to Research Specialists \***

| Function | Number Specifying | Number Finding Inadequately Performed |
|---|---|---|
| Identifying problems of research | 39 | 11 |
| Making judgments on data | 39 | 9 |
| Providing data through own observations, records, etc. | 37 | 3 |
| Collecting data | 34 | 1 |
| Making recommendations on basis of research findings | 33 | 8 |
| Formulating problems into researchable questions | 32 | 27 |
| Participating in interdisciplinary team conducting research | 32 | 1 |
| Evaluating significance of research questions for practice | 30 | 8 |
| Translating research findings into practice | 30 | 11 |
| Developing data collecting instruments | 28 | 20 |
| Interpreting data to research staff | 27 | 5 |
| Classifying data | 24 | 7 |
| Analyzing data | 24 | 15 |
| Preparing research design | 23 | 21 |
| Reporting research findings | 21 | 9 |
| Formulating research policy | 18 | 7 |
| Planning administration of research project | 17 | 6 |
| Testing results of research | 15 | 7 |

\* Based on response of 46 research specialists selected from members of the Social Work Research Section of NASW who have had contact with social work practitioners in research projects.

TABLE III

## Opinions of Research Specialists on Content of Research Sequence for Practitioners *

| Content | Number considering content essential for practitioners | | | |
|---|---|---|---|---|
| | Participating in research | | Other roles of practitioner | |
| Significance of scientific inquiry | 36 | (6) | 38 | (1) |
| Characteristics of scientific method | 46 | (1) | 31 | (3) |
| Relationship of social work to social science | 26 | (13) | 21 | (6) |
| Problems of research in social phenomena | 29 | (9) | 11 | (16) |
| Nature of social work knowledge | 28 | (11) | 32 | (2) |
| Functions and objectives of research in social work | 42 | (2) | 26 | (5) |
| Relationship of research and practice in social work | 40 | (3) | 27 | (4) |
| History and development of social work research | 5 | (30) | 5 | (26) |
| Current research in social work and related fields | 32 | (7) | 16 | (9) |
| Organization and administration of social work research | 15 | (27) | 10 | (22) |
| Formulation of research problems | 39 | (4) | 15 | (10) |
| Research design | 22 | (19) | 5 | (28) |
| Sources of data for research | 21 | (22) | 12 | (15) |
| Methods of data collection | 26 | (15) | 12 | (13) |
| Organization and classification of data | 21 | (22) | 11 | (20) |
| Data analysis | 21 | (24) | 9 | (24) |

TABLE III—*Continued*

| Content | Number considering content essential for practitioners | |
|---|---|---|
| | Participating in research | Other roles of practitioner |
| Conclusion drawing | 38 (5) | 11 (18) |
| Report writing | 22 (20) | 12 (13) |
| Techniques of scholarly practice | 15 (26) | 8 (25) |
| Frequency distribution | 26 (16) | 13 (12) |
| Averages | 27 (12) | 18 (8) |
| Variability | 23 (17) | 9 (23) |
| Association | 19 (25) | 5 (27) |
| Time series | 9 (29) | 5 (29) |
| Sampling | 26 (14) | 11 (19) |
| Reliability and significance | 28 (10) | 10 (20) |
| Graphic presentation | 13 (28) | 4 (30) |
| Statistics on social services | 22 (21) | 14 (11) |
| Analysis of social service statistics | 23 (18) | 11 (17) |
| Application of statistics to welfare problems | 30 (8) | 20 (7) |

* Based on responses of 46 research specialists selected from members of the Social Work Research Section of NASW who have had contact with social work practitioners in research projects. Numbers in parentheses represent relative position of items as to essentiality.

TABLE IV

## Content of Courses in Research Curricula of Schools of Social Work for Practitioners of Methods other than Social Work Research

| Content of Courses | Number of Schools |
|---|---|
| Methods of problem-solving | 3 |
| Nature of science | 5 |
| Concepts and principles of scientific inquiry | 16 |
| Scientific method in research and social work practice | 6 |
| Nature of social work knowledge | 3 |
| Relationship of social work to the social sciences and other disciplines | 11 |
| Function and purpose of research in social work | 18 |
| History and development of research in social work | 5 |
| Organization of research in social work | 5 |
| Problems in conducting research in social work | 9 |
| Relationship of research to practice | 12 |
| Administration of research in social work agencies | 7 |
| Types of studies conducted in social work research | 12 |
| Current research in social work | 3 |
| Criteria for evaluating research | 1 |
| Sources of social work research | 2 |
| Sources of data for social work knowledge | 8 |
| Research design | 15 |
| Methods of data collection | 23 |
| Classification and organization of data | 16 |
| Analysis of data | 7 |
| Reporting of findings | 11 |
| Sampling techniques | 11 |
| Statistics | 35 |
| Social bookkeeping and agency statistics | 4 |

SOURCES: School catalogs, course outlines and other curriculum materials.

9-77-1

## DATE DUE

| | | | |
|---|---|---|---|
| | | | |
| | | | |
| | | | |
| | | | |
| | | | |
| | | | |
| | | | |
| | | | |
| | | | |
| | | | |
| | | | |
| | | | |
| | | | |
| | | | |
| | | | |
| | | | |